Akathist
to
Saint Paisius of Neamt

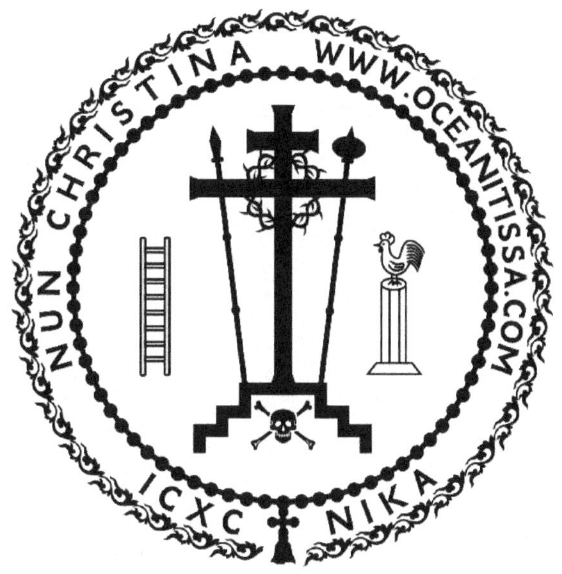

Anna Skoubourdis
Nun Christina

Published by: Virgin Mary of Australia and Oceania 2022 ©
oceanitissa@gmail.com
www.oceanitissa.com.au
Youtube: Nun Christina Oceanitissa

Subscribe to receive updates and Orthodox Christian creative media

www.oceanitissa.com

Venerable Païsios Velichkovsky

Troparion & Kontakion

Commemorated on November 15

Troparion — Tone 2

Having become a stranger on earth, / you reached the heavenly homeland, O Venerable Father Païsios. / You taught the faithful to lift up their minds to God, / crying out to Him with all their hearts: / "Lord Jesus Christ, Son of God, have mercy on me, a sinner."

Kontakion — Tone 8

Like a much-laboring bee, you were an elect zealot of the monastic life, / supplying our souls with the writings of the Fathers, through which you guide us on the path of salvation. / Therefore, we cry out to you: "Hail, truly wise Païsios, / for through you, the tradition of spiritual Elders has been restored to us!"

Akathist

Kontakion 1:

Blessed Father, following Christ, you left your parent's house and, finding no rest in your homeland, you became a hermit on Mount Athos; and, like another Abraham, you've settled in the blessed Romanian land, becoming a great abbot and Father, with many spiritual sons in the land of Moldavia. For this, we piously cry to you: Rejoice, Pious Father Paisius, great advisor of monks!

Ikos 1:

Born into a family of priests, you loved Christ from childhood and desired peace and unceasing prayer, for which we ask you to receive from us, your sons, this song of praise:
Rejoice, chosen vessel of the Holy Spirit;
Rejoice, precious flower of Poltava;
Rejoice, spiritual lily of Orthodoxy;
Rejoice, for you were called by Christ as a child;
Rejoice, for you have loved the Church since childhood;
Rejoice, torch that burns for the Lord;
Rejoice, unextinguished candle of the East;
Rejoice, lit candle of prayer;
Rejoice, pure candlestick of virginity;
Rejoice, dwelling of heavenly delights;
Rejoice, young man with the mind of an elder;
Rejoice, wise elder with a parent's heart;
Rejoice, Reverend Father Paisius, great advisor of monks!

Kontakion 2:

Neither the tears of your mother, nor the longing of your brothers, nor your native motherland could stop you from following Christ, but, by forsaking them all, you conquered the devils and the temptations of youth and left your friends, running towards the heavenly, blessed things, for which together with you we sing to Christ: Alleluia!

Icos 2:

We marvel at your zeal, saint, at how you left the transient for the eternal; how you overcame the weaknesses of nature and found shelter in a foreign land, becoming a spiritual son of the Pious Basil of Poiana Mărului and a skilled hermit at the Holy Mount Athos, for which we sing to you:
Rejoice, chosen stone of faith;
Rejoice, fruitful olive tree of the Church;
Rejoice, tall cedar in the garden of Heaven;
Rejoice, apple watered by the dew of the Holy Spirit;
Rejoice, fruitful vine;
Rejoice, land of many fruits;
Rejoice, grace-bearing grain of wheat;
Rejoice, fragrant rose of the Church;
Rejoice, fruit untouched by passion;
Rejoice, pure soul of a heavenly child;
Rejoice, spiritual father with many sons;
Rejoice, skilled teacher of sleepless prayer;
Rejoice, Reverend Father Paisius, great advisor of monks!

Kontakion 3:

The fathers from the Dălhăuți and Poiana Mărului monasteries were amazed, seeing your zeal for prayer and obedience, the deep humility of your heart, and the tears that flowed from your eyes. But you, Father, hiding everything in the chamber of your soul, sang unceasingly to Christ: Alleluia!

Ikos 3:

You have followed Christ from childhood, having God as your Father, the Church as your mother, and the Blessed Virgin Mary as your protection, the saints and angels as your brothers, and the Reverends of Athos and the priests from the monasteries of Moldavia as your guides. For this, we faithfully cry out to you:
Rejoice, citizen of Heaven;
Rejoice, speaker with the angels;
Rejoice, spiritual son of Mount Athos;
Rejoice, long-sought abbot of the Atonites;
Rejoice, for you were called by Christ to the land of Moldovia;
Rejoice, for you did not oppose the divine will;

Rejoice, for you loved nothing earthly;
Rejoice, for you have found rest and abode for your sons in the Dragomirna Monastery;
Rejoice, for you have gathered multitude of souls in it;
Rejoice, worthy servant of the King Christ;
Rejoice, for you have fed the monks with divine teachings;
Rejoice, holy bearer of light;
Rejoice, Reverend Father Paisius, great advisor of monks!

Kontakion 4:

How shall we praise your plight, Reverend Father? For we marvel at your zeal for doing good deeds, your strength in toil, your patience in all-night vigil, your secret tears, and your gift of unceasing prayer that rested in your heart. Therefore, please, help us with your gift to walk the path of repentance and to sing to God: Alleluia!

Ikos 4:

We know you as a father among fathers and a teacher among teachers, Pious Father Paisius; a skilled priest with just measure, a wise abbot and father of thousands of monks, and a great supplicant before the Most Holy Trinity. Therefore, with great reverence, we sing to you:
Rejoice, unwavering pillar of the right faith;
Rejoice, immutable frontier of truth;
Rejoice, hard rock of orthodox dogmas;
Rejoice, humble thinker to the heavenly things;
Rejoice, skillful teacher of good deeds;
Rejoice, unextinguished candle of holy prayer;
Rejoice, guiding star of monks;
Rejoice, renewer of the Dragomirna Monastery;
Rejoice, father of the poor and doctor of the sick;
Rejoice, interpreter of the Philokalia;
Rejoice, loving friend of the Holy Fathers;
Rejoice, servant of the Holy Trinity;
Rejoice, Reverend Father Paisius, great advisor of monks!

Kontakion 5:

Following Christ and His saints in everything, you loved the prayer and teachings of the divine Fathers the most. This is why, Blessed one, you founded three spiritual cities of unceasing prayer in Moldova, the Dragomirna, Secu, and Neamțu monasteries, making this country the second Orthodox Athos. For this, together with the angels, we sing to God: Alleluia!

Ikos 5:

Holy Father Paisius, we marvel at the gifts you received from Christ, the humility and gentleness of your heart, and the care you had for the Orthodox people persecuted by those of a different law, for which we sing to you:
Rejoice, holy teacher of prayer;
Rejoice, chosen disciple of the Holy Fathers;
Rejoice, secret chamber of the Holy Spirit;
Rejoice, father of monastic groups;
Rejoice, defender of the poor and the persecuted;
Rejoice, dweller in heaven with the saints;
Rejoice, tireless servant of the Holy Liturgy;
Rejoice, never-sleeping eye and ever-awake mind;
Rejoice, expeller of devils;
Rejoice, harsh rebuker of the lazy;
Rejoice, hasty helper of the afflicted;
Rejoice, wise priest of Moldavia;
Rejoice, Reverend Father Paisius, great advisor of monks!

Kontakion 6:

Reverend Father, after the fall of Bukovina in foreigners' hands, you went to the Secu Monastery, halving the community of your sons, and, with hot tears parting from them, you settled here, Father, gathering other disciples around you and together with them, you glorified God incessantly, singing: Alleluia!

Ikos 6:

Laboring at the Secu Monastery, you filled the mountains and valleys with hermits and pious ones, renewing the hermitages of Sihla and

Sihăstria to the praise of God, for which, blessed one, receive this song:
Rejoice, abode of prayer;
Rejoice, house of blessing;
Rejoice, supplicant of the Most Holy Trinity;
Rejoice, praise of the Mother of God;
Rejoice, candle of the Church;
Rejoice, teacher of repentance;
Rejoice, father of the hermits;
Rejoice, living Church of divine love;
Rejoice, you who talked to angels;
Rejoice, you who prayed with the fathers;
Rejoice, you who lived with the saints;
Rejoice, faithful servant of Christ;
Rejoice, Reverend Father Paisius, great advisor of monks!

Kontakion 7:

You did not allow your eyes to sleep, Reverend Father, nor your lashes, for day and night you prayed for yourself and your sons to be delivered from the enemy's traps, singing to God with them: Alleluia!

Ikos 7:

Being a vessel of prayer and a tree of Heaven, you received grace and comfort from above through the intercession of the Mother of God and all the saints, whom you faithfully followed, for whom we cry to you:
Rejoice, pillar of prayer;
Rejoice, pleasant-smelling incense;
Rejoice, divine myrrh;
Rejoice, angelic image;
Rejoice, spiritual father;
Rejoice, torch that lights the path of life;
Rejoice, flame that burns devils;
Rejoice, chamber where you talk to Christ;
Rejoice, healer of spiritual and physical diseases;
Rejoice, skillful teacher of the young;
Rejoice, humble counselor of the elders;
Rejoice, for your are shadowed by the Holy Spirit;

Rejoice, Reverend Father Paisius, great advisor of monks!

Kontakion 8:

God's providence called you to Neamţ, Holy Father Paisius, where you came with your sons from the Secu Monastery in teary eyes to increase the spiritual life in Christ, to Whom we sing: Alleluia!

Ikos 8:

You were received with great joy in the Neamţ Monastery where, with prayers and all-nigh vigils, glorifying the Father, the Son, and the Holy Spirit, God, you labored, for which we joyfully cry out to you:
Rejoice, wise shepherd of Neamţ Monastery;
Rejoice, first among the abbots of Moldavia;
Rejoice, sleepless and foresightful eye;
Rejoice, counselor of hierarchs and rulers;
Rejoice, skilled renewer of the monastic life;
Rejoice, defender of spiritual life;
Rejoice, father of pious fathers;
Rejoice, scale of righteous judgment;
Rejoice, fountain of living water;
Rejoice, fire that burns all temptations;
Rejoice, founder of many hermitages;
Rejoice, guide of the hermits of Mount Ceahlău;
Rejoice, Reverend Father Paisius, great advisor of monks!

Kontakion 9:

Holy Father Paisius, how can we be silent and not reveal your deeds and praise your secret labors? For, adding hardships upon hardships, sprinkling them with many tears and gathering around you a multitude of monks, you made the Neamţ and Secu Monasteries earthly heaven and spiritual heaven; for these, we bring praise to the Holy Trinity, singing: Alleluia!

Ikos 9:

Venerable Father, we praise your life and honor the multitudes of monks gathered around you, who continually glorified God with spiritual chants and angelic voices; for all loved you, all followed you and with joy longed for Christ, for which, together with them, we cry out to you:
Rejoice, father of the prayer of the heart;
Rejoice, bright torch of the Orthodox;
Rejoice, renewer of many monasteries;
Rejoice, adviser of the Optina Monastery;
Rejoice, spiritual founder of the Văratic Monastery;
Rejoice, precious ornament of Moldavia and Wallachia;
Rejoice, holy priest of monks and hermits;
Rejoice, friend of the saints and the pious;
Rejoice, wise guide of Christian rulers and officials;
Rejoice, pillar of trust of the weak and powerless;
Rejoice, tireless fighter against passions;
Rejoice, sword that cuts evil thoughts;
Rejoice, Reverend Father Paisius, great advisor of monks!

Kontakion 10:

Reverend Father, the spiritual shepherds sought you, monks and hermits followed your advice, the sick in body and soul received health and blessing from you; you fed the poor, and no one left you deprived and uncomforted; for this, with joy, together with you and your sons, we sing to Christ God: Alleluia!

Ikos 10:

Your name became known in all the Orthodox countries, and many ran to the community of the Neamț Monastery, wanting to follow your life or at least to see and listen to you. For the priests asked for your advice, the rulers asked for a blessing, the monks followed your exhortations, and the poor returned with mercy; for which we, together with them, offer this hymn of praise:
Rejoice, fortified stronghold of Orthodoxy;
Rejoice, joy of the monks;
Rejoice, morning star of the hermits;
Rejoice, advisor of the rulers;
Rejoice, counselor of hierarchs;

Rejoice, comforter of the faithful;
Rejoice, crown of the Neamţ and Secu Monasteries;
Rejoice, teacher and foreseer;
Rejoice, kind and forgiving parent;
Rejoice, teacher of holiness;
Rejoice, fervent supplicant for us all;
Rejoice, precious torch of Moldavia;
Rejoice, Reverend Father Paisius, great advisor of monks!

Kontakion 11:

Loving Christ and the teachings of His saints, you made the Neamţ Monastery a place of worship, a fortified wall against passions, and a school of spirituality, filling Moldova with the teachings of the Holy Fathers and guiding everyone on the path of salvation; therefore, in one voice, we sing to God: Alleluia!

Ikos 11:

Holy Father Paisius, approaching your death, sadness gripped everyone and moving to heaven accompanied by angels, you were counted among the Holy Fathers, leaving your sons in tears, with whom we cry out to you:
Rejoice, friend of the saints;
Rejoice, angels' joy;
Rejoice, for you were counted among the saints;
Rejoice, dweller of Paradise;
Rejoice, citizen of Heaven;
Rejoice, you who sing the praises to God;
Rejoice, candle of Orthodoxy;
Rejoice, for your name is known to all;
Rejoice, for you pray to Christ for us all;
Rejoice, for you are crowned by the Holy Spirit;
Rejoice, Holy Father, our advisor;
Rejoice, for you live in the light of Christ;
Rejoice, Reverend Father Paisius, great advisor of monks!

Kontakion 12:

Your honorable tomb, in the church of the Neamț Monastery, and your holy relics comfort us and help us all with the power of your prayers to God. Therefore, Holy Father Paisius, pray for us so that we may obtain forgiveness of sins and sing together to Christ God: Alleluia!

Ikos 12:

As a skilled priest, you came to us, and as an angel in the flesh, you went to God, Reverend Father Paisius, leaving your spiritual sons grieved. For this, pray to the Most Holy Trinity to protect us from all the evil on earth and to make us heirs of the heavenly kingdom so that together, in one voice, we may sing this hymn to you:
Rejoice, earthly angel and heavenly man;
Rejoice, son of Ukraine and father of Moldavia;
Rejoice, praise of Poltava and joy of Orthodoxy;
Rejoice, torch of Mount Athos and father of monks;
Rejoice, for you live with all the saints in heaven,
Rejoice, disciple of the Reverend Basil from Poiana Mărului;
Rejoice, for you were an ascetic with the hermit Onufrie from Voronei Hermitage;
Rejoice, Pious, for you lived and interpreted the Philokalia;
Rejoice, for you have left us your faith and works as a testament;
Rejoice, for together with the angels, you sing to the Most Holy Trinity;
Rejoice, precious child of Orthodox monasticism;
Rejoice, fervent intercessor for us to God;
Rejoice, Reverend Father Paisius, great advisor of monks!

Kontakion 13:

O Reverend Father Paisius, the crown of Orthodox monasticism, holy abbot and spiritual father, adornment of the Church and heir of the heavenly kingdom, receive these humble prayers from us, your unworthy sons, who sing together with the angels: Alleluia! (repeat three times)

Repeat Ikos 1 and Kontakion 1.

Ikos 1:

Born into a family of priests, you loved Christ from childhood and desired peace and unceasing prayer, for which we ask you to receive from us, your sons, this song of praise:
Rejoice, chosen vessel of the Holy Spirit;
Rejoice, precious flower of Poltava;
Rejoice, spiritual lily of Orthodoxy;
Rejoice, for you were called by Christ as a child;
Rejoice, for you have loved the Church since childhood;
Rejoice, torch that burns for the Lord;
Rejoice, unextinguished candle of the East;
Rejoice, lit candle of prayer;
Rejoice, pure candlestick of virginity;
Rejoice, dwelling of heavenly delights;
Rejoice, young man with the mind of an elder;
Rejoice, wise elder with a parent's heart;
Rejoice, Reverend Father Paisius, great advisor of monks!

Kontakion 1:

Blessed Father, following Christ, you left your parent's house and, finding no rest in your homeland, you became a hermit on Mount Athos; and, like another Abraham, you've settled in the blessed Romanian land, becoming a great abbot and Father, with many spiritual sons in the land of Moldavia. For this, we piously cry to you:
Rejoice, Pious Father Paisius, great advisor of monks!

Prayer to our Reverend Father Paisius of Neamț

Reverend Father Paisius, son of Ukraine and spiritual father of Moldavia, praise of Orthodox monasticism, holy abbot of Neamț Monastery, father and teacher of the unceasing prayer, and gentle and humble advisor of pious monks, we kneel with reverence before your holy icon and faithfully ask you to pray before the Holy Trinity for us sinners, your sons.

Hear our prayers and take them to Christ and the Blessed Virgin Mary. Remove the heavy temptations from us, and help us with your prayers to overcome our evil passions and thoughts. Teach us, Holy Father Paisius, to pray with tears; teach us to love and glorify God unceasingly. Drive away from us the tempest of bodily and spiritual temptations, disobedience, pride, and every cunning thought. Strengthen the spiritual life in our monasteries and, above all, humility, obedience, and holy prayer.

Deliver us from the weakening of faith and the hardening of the heart, and pray to the Lord to give us good spiritual fathers and the gift of holy tears so that, living in humility and pure life, we may acquire the heavenly kingdom that Christ promised us. Pray, Reverend Father Paisius, together with all the saints, so that Christ may strengthen the true faith in the world and holy life in monasteries, villages, and cities everywhere.

Help us, Reverend Father Paisius, to fulfill the commandments of Christ, and pray together with the heavenly hosts for our hierarchic fathers, priests, and monks, for mothers and children, for those who are in suffering and need, and for all the faithful Christians and for the peace of the Church of Christ, to protect us from all evil with the grace of the Most Holy Trinity, to Whom praise and thanksgiving are due forever and ever. Amen.

Biography

Saint Païsios Velichkovsky was born in Poltava in Little Russia on December 21, 1722, and was the eleventh of twelve children. His father John was a priest, who named him Peter at his Baptism, in honor of Saint Peter the Metropolitan of Moscow, on whose Feast he was born.

After the children's father died, their mother Irene raised them in piety. Peter was sent to study at the Moghila Academy in Kiev in 1735. After four years, Peter decided to leave the world and become a monk. At the age of seventeen, he went in search of a monastery and a good Spiritual Father. For seven years Peter visited various monasteries, including the Kiev Caves Lavra, but he did not feel drawn to any of the monasteries of Ukraine.

After being made a rassophore monk (one blessed to wear the rasson, but not yet tonsured "into the mantya") at the Saint Nicholas Medvedevsky Monastery with the name Platon, he found that there was no experienced Elder there who could teach him obedience, or give him spiritual direction. Not wishing to begin his monastic life without such guidance, he left the monastery a week afterward with the blessing of his Elder.

At first, he went to Kiev, where he happened to meet his sister-in-law, the widow of his older brother Archpriest John. She informed him of his mother's sorrow when he left Kiev, and her mind seemed to be affected by her grief. Then one day an Angel appeared to her and told her that instead of loving the Creator with all her heart and soul, she loved His creation (her son) more. Because of this excessive love, the Angel continued, she was thinking of starving herself to death, which would result in her eternal condemnation. The Angel said that by God's grace, her son would become a monk, and that she should also renounce the world and become a nun. After this, she became calm and accepted God's will. She entered a convent and was tonsured with the name Juliana. After ten years or so, she departed to the Lord.

While at Kiev, Father Platon met two monks from Romania who were about to return to their country. After crossing the border into

Moldavia, they came to Vlachia and the Skete of Saint Nicholas, which is called Trăisteni, around 1745. The Elder of the Skete, Hieroschema-monk Michael, was away on business in Ukraine, so Father Platon and his companions were welcomed by the Superior, Father Dēmētrios. Father Platon was placed under a general obedience and was given a cell near the Skete, from which the church was visible.

As he was sleeping one night, the semantron was sounded calling the monks to Sunday Matins, but Father Platon did not hear it. He woke up and ran to the church, only to find that the Gospel had already been read, and the Canon was being sung. In his grief and shame, he did not enter the church, but returned to his cell, weeping bitter tears. After the Liturgy, when it was time for the meal, the Superior and the Elder were surprised that Father Platon had not been seen at the Services. The Elder ordered that the meal be delayed while he sent Father Athanasios to find out what had happened to the absent monk.. Father Athanasios found him and asked why he was weeping. With difficulty, Father Platon was able to tell him the reason for his sorrow. Father Athanasios tried to console him and urged him to come to the Skete, where the others were waiting for him. Finally, he was persuaded to go.

Seeing the brethren at table but not eating, Father Platon fell down before them weeping and asking their forgiveness. The Elder and the Superior lraised him up and heard from Father Athanasios the reason for his sorrow. The Elder told Father Platon not to grieve so over something that had happened involuntarily, and did his best to console him. From that time, however, the Saint would not sleep lying down in bed, but sitting up on a bench.

One day the Elder Onuphrios of Kyrkoul visited the Skete and spoke about his Skete at Kyrkoul. Father Platon longed to see Kyrkoul, and so he returned there with Father Onuphrios. He remained there for a time, conversing with Father Onuphrius about overcoming the passions, the struggle with demons, unceasing prayer, and other soul-profiting topics. This seed fell on good ground, and later produced spiritual fruit a hundredfold (Luke 8:8).

The time came when Father Platon was filled with longing to visit Mount Athos. He asked the brethren of the Skete, and those of other Sketes, for their forgiveness and blessing for the journey. He also thanked them for their kindness and their paternal instruction. They blessed him and let him go in peace. At that time, he was just twenty-four years old.

Father Platon went to Mount Athos in 1746, arriving at the Greatest Lavra on July 4, the eve of the Feast of Saint Athanasios of Athos. His traveling companion, Hieromonk Tryphon fell ill and reposed after four days. Father Platon would have died from the same illness, if not for the care of the Russian monks. He recovered and lived in solitude in a cell called Kaparis near the Pantokrator Monastery. He went around visiting many ascetics and solitaries, seeking a Spiritual Father, but was unable to find anyone suitable.

In 1750 Saint Basil of Poiana Mărului (April 15) visited the Holy Mountain and spent some time with Father Platon, who asked him for monastic tonsure. Elder Basil granted his request, giving him the name Païsios. Then Father Basil returned to his Skete at Vlachia. About three months later, a young monk named Bessarion came to the Holy Mountain from Vlachia. He went around to the monasteries searching for an instructor, but did not find one. He also came to Father Païsios and asked him to tell him something about saving his soul. Father Païsios sighed and told him that he himself had been looking for an instructor without success. Yet, feeling compassion for Father Bessarion, he talked to him a little about the qualifications necessary for a true instructor, and about the Jesus Prayer. After hearing him, Father Bessarion said, “Why should I seek any further?" He fell down at the feet of Father Païsios, entreating him to be his Elder. Father Païsios did not wish to be anyone’s Elder, preferring to be one under the authority of an Elder. Father Bessarion wept for three days until Father Païsios finally agreed to accept him as a friend, but not as a disciple. They lived together for about four years, fulfilling God’s commandments, cutting off their own will, and obeying one another as equals.

Other disciples began to join them, and their number continued to increase. Since they needed a priest and a confessor, they pleaded with Father Païsios to accept ordination. He did not want to hear of this, and repeatedly refused to consent. They did not give up, however. They asked him how he could expect to teach the brethren obedience and cutting off their own will, when he disobeyed the tearful entreaties of those who wished him to accept. Finally, he said, "May God's will be done."

In 1754 Father Païsios was ordained to the holy priesthood and was given the Skete of the Prophet Elias, where he began to accept even more disciples. Saint Païsios remained on Mount Athos for seventeen years, copying Greek patristic books and translating them into Slavonic.

In 1763 Father Païsios went to Moldavia with sixty-four disciples, and was given the Dragomírna Monastery near the city of Sochava, on the border between Bukovina and Moldavia. Here he remained for twelve years, and the number of monks increased to three hundred and fifty. His friend Hieromonk Alexius came to visit him from Vlachia, and Father Païsios asked to be tonsured into the Schema. Father Alexius did so, but without changing his name. While at Dragomírna, Elder Païsios corrected the Slavonic translations of patristic books by comparing them to the Greek manuscripts he had copied on Mount Athos.

The Russo-Turkish War broke out in 1768, and Moldavia and Vlachia saw many battles. Dragomírna and the forests around it became filled with refugees from the villages near the battlegrounds. Another catastrophe followed in 1771 with an outbreak of the plague. When Dragomírna and Bukovina came under the control of Austrian Catholics, so Saint Païsios and his flock fled to Moldavia. In October of 1775, the Holy Elder and many of his monks went to Secu Monastery, which is dedicated to the Beheading of Saint John the Baptist.

Secu was too small for the number of brethren, who were crowded with three to five monks in a cell. In the spring, more brethren were due to arrive from Dragomírna, so new cells had to be built. After three years of labor one hundred cells were completed, and everyone had a place. Still, the numbers continued to increase, and they had to look for a larger monastery.

Prince Constantine Muruz wrote to the Elder saying that there was no larger monastery than Neamţ, about two hours from Secu. On August 14, 1779, Saint Païsios moved to Neamţ Monastery, where he spent the last fifteen years of his life translating the writings of the Holy Fathers. He also introduced the the Typikon (Rule) of Mount Athos in that community. He gathered about a thousand monks in the monastery, instructing them in the unceasing prayer of the heart.

Archbishop Ambrose visited Saint Païsios at Neamţ in 1790, remaining for two days to converse with the Elder. During the Sunday Liturgy, he raised Saint Païsios to the rank of Archimandrite. He stayed for two more days, then departed after blessing everyone.

Saint Païsios fell asleep in the Lord on November 15, 1794 when he was almost seventy-two. It is possible that God revealed the time of his death to him beforehand, for he stopped translating books. He merely reviewed and corrected what had already been translated.

He was ill for four days, but felt well enough to attend the Liturgy on Sunday. After the service, he asked everyone to come and receive his blessing. Bidding farewell to them all, he returned to his cell and would not receive anyone. A few days later, on November 15, he received the Holy Mysteries once more, and surrendered his soul to God. His funeral was conducted by Bishop Benjamin of Tuma, and was attended by multitudes of priests, monks, laymen, nobles and ordinary people.

The holy relics of Saint Païsios were uncovered in 1846, 1853, 1861 and 1872, and were found to be incorrupt.

Saint Païsios has had an enormous influence, not only in Romania, but throughout the Orthodox world. His disciples traveled to Russia, sparking the spiritual revival of the XIX century with Slavonic translations of the Philokalia and the tradition of eldership which they had learned from Saint Païsios. His influence has been felt even in America, through Saint Herman of Alaska (December 13). Saint Herman had been taught by Elders whose spiritual formation was guided by Saint Païsios.

While he was still in Russia, Saint Herman met Saint Nazarius (February 23), who became his Elder at Valaam, at Sarov, then followed him to Sanaxar Monastery when Saint Theodore (February 19) was the Igoumen. One of the books that Saint Herman brought with him to America was the Slavonic Philokalia, printed in 1794. Not only did he absorb the spiritual wisdom that it contained, he also imparted it to others.

Books published by Nun Christina Oceanitissa:

The collective works of St Nektarios of Aegina.
The Philokalia 5: The full text in English.
The collective works of Elder Cleopa.
The Anacreontic Poems by Saint Sophronius Patriarch of Jerusalem.
The Life of Saint Paul of Thebes the First Hermit.
The Devil: The Cause of Sin by Saint John of Kronstadt.
Faith and the Orthodox Church by Saint John of Kronstadt.
The Monastic Rule of Saint Pachomius the Great.
Supplicatory Canon and Akathist to St Paisios.
Supplicatory Canon and Akathist to St Porphyrios.
Supplicatory Canon and Akathist to St George.
Supplicatory Canon and Akathist to St Anastasia.
Supplicatory Canon and Akathist to St Anna.
Supplicatory Canon and Akathist to St John the Russian.
Supplicatory Canon and Akathist to St Ephraim of Nea Makri.
Supplicatory Canon and Akathist to St John Maximovitch.
Supplicatory Canon and Akathist to St Dimitri.
Supplicatory Canon and Akathist to St Joseph the Hesycast.
Supplicatory Canon and Akathist to St Luke the Surgeon.
Supplicatory Canon and Akathist to St John the Baptist.
The Way of a Pilgrim.
Conversation with a Grieving Man by St Dimitri of Rostov.
The Inner Man by St Dimitri of Rostov.
Orthodox Prayer Book.
Daily Orthodox Prayer book.

Books published by [illegible] Christian Republica.

The [illegible] Works of [illegible] Nektarios of Aegina
[illegible]
[illegible]
[illegible] Patriarchs [illegible] Jerusalem
The [illegible] of [illegible]
The [illegible] Saint John of [illegible]
The Menaion [illegible] the Cross
Supplementary Canon [illegible] to St Patrick
[illegible]
Supplementary Canon and Akathist to St Anastasia
Supplementary Canon and Akathist to St [illegible]
Supplementary Canon [illegible] to St [illegible]
Supplementary Canon [illegible] to St [illegible]
[illegible]
Supplementary Canon [illegible] St [illegible]

www.ingramcontent.com/pod-product-compliance
Lightning Source LLC
LaVergne TN
LVHW010512160826
845677LV00012B/2815

* 9 7 9 8 8 4 6 3 5 5 4 9 1 *